Zeitgeist
für OCR 1

Self Study Guide

Miriam Friedmann

OXFORD
UNIVERSITY PRESS

Great Clarendon Street, Oxford OX2 6DP

Oxford University Press is a department of the University of Oxford.
It furthers the University's objective of excellence in research, scholarship,
and education by publishing worldwide in

Oxford   New York
Auckland   Cape Town   Dar es Salaam   Hong Kong   Karachi
Kuala Lumpur   Madrid   Melbourne   Mexico City   Nairobi
New Delhi   Shanghai   Taipei   Toronto

With offices in

Argentina   Austria   Brazil   Chile   Czech Republic   France   Greece
Guatemala   Hungary   Italy   Japan   South Korea   Poland   Portugal
Singapore   Switzerland   Thailand   Turkey   Ukraine   Vietnam

Oxford is a registered trade mark of Oxford University Press
in the UK and in certain other countries

British Library Cataloguing in Publication Data

Data available

ISBN 978 019 915375 6

  3 5 7 9 10 8 6 4 2

Typeset by Thomson

Printed in Great Britain by Martins the Printers

Acknowledgements

The author and publisher would like to thank Melissa Weir (project
manager) and Marion Dill (language consultant).

Contents

General Exam Tips

Here's a reminder of the topics you have studied for AS Level and which you now need to revise.

Aspects of Daily Life

▶ The family: structure and relationships; living conditions

▶ Food, drink, health, addictions

▶ Transport

Leisure and Entertainment

▶ Sport (including national sporting concerns and traditions)

▶ Tourism and related themes

▶ Leisure activities e.g. pastimes, music, films, theatre

Communication and Media

▶ Communication technology

▶ Media, e.g. written press, radio, television

Education and Training

▶ School and school life

▶ Work and training

You will be taking two examinations:

Unit 1: The Speaking Test

The Speaking Test is worth **30%** of your AS grade (and **15%** of the full A Level).
The test lasts 15 minutes and you have 20 minutes to prepare beforehand.
You are not allowed to use a dictionary.

There are two sections:

▶ A role play

▶ Discussion of topics

Unit 2: The Listening, Reading and Writing Paper

This paper is worth **70%** of your AS Level (and **35%** of the full A Level) and the time allowed is two hours and 15 minutes.

There are two sections:

▶ Listening and Writing

▶ Reading and Writing

Pass grades for this examination range from A down to E. Here's an idea of what you need to be able to do.

If you pass AS Level German with an A grade, it means you can:

▶ Clearly understand spoken language, including details and people's opinions.

▶ Work out what someone is trying to say even if they don't spell it out in detail.

▶ Clearly understand written texts, understanding both the gist and the details.

▶ Talk fluently, giving your opinions and justifying them, and using a good range of vocabulary and generally accurate pronunciation.

▶ Organise your ideas and write them up well in German.

▶ Write using a wide range of vocabulary and grammatical structures without making many mistakes.

If you pass AS Level German with an E grade, it means you:

▶ Show some understanding of spoken German, even if you have difficulties when the language is complex and miss some of the details.

▶ Can sometimes work out what someone is trying to say even if they don't give all the details.

▶ Understand straightforward written texts, although you don't always understand more difficult writing.

▶ Can talk in German, and convey basic information, perhaps a little hesitantly and relying on material you have learned by heart. There is probably some English influence on your pronunciation.

▶ Can convey information in writing, perhaps with some difficulty in organising your material and expressing it.

▶ Use a range of vocabulary and structures, but quite often you make mistakes.

Preparing for the exams

You can see from these lists that when planning your revision there are really six areas you need to practise:

▶ Speaking
▶ Listening
▶ Reading
▶ Writing
▶ Vocabulary
▶ Grammar

There are tips on how to prepare each area overleaf.

Speaking

▶ Take every opportunity to practise speaking German – in lessons, with the language assistant, with a friend, with anyone you know who speaks German.

▶ Take an oral question from your textbook and work out a few sentences to answer it, then record them on tape and listen to see what areas still need practice – perhaps fluency, pronunciation or good use of vocabulary and structures.

▶ Don't write everything down first. You won't have a script on the day! You can write a few key words down for reference, but definitely no full sentences.

Listening

▶ Keep listening to German, ideally every day. Use a mix of extracts you have worked on and new texts.

▶ Try listening to something for which you have the transcript. Just listen first, then listen again with the transcript and, if necessary, look up unknown words. Finally, listen again without the transcript and challenge yourself to understand everything.

▶ Watching films is excellent listening practice and watching more than once is even better! Try watching with the subtitles and then without. If you find this hard going, just re-watch a short extract.

▶ German radio and TV programmes are useful, but can also be difficult. Record an extract and listen or watch it more than once. You will find it gets easier.

▶ Make sure you do some exam listening practice too!

Reading

▶ Keep reading a mix of things you read once quickly, such as a magazine, and things where you work hard at a short passage and try to understand everything. Texts from your textbook are useful for this.

▶ It's useful to note new vocabulary from your reading, but don't make it such hard work that you give up. Note, say, three new words from each text.

▶ Try a 'dual-language' reading book, where you get the original German on one page and an English translation on the opposite one. This is an excellent way to practise reading longer texts without losing heart!

▶ Search on the internet for articles in German on any topic which interests you.

Writing

▶ Practise planning essay questions. Jot down ideas for each paragraph – in German! – along with key vocabulary.

▶ Take a key paragraph from a piece of marked work, write some English prompts to remind you of its content and then write it out from memory. Concentrate especially on sections where the teacher suggested improvements.

▶ Look carefully at marked work and identify what grammar errors you are making. Then check them up in a grammar book and try some practice exercises.

▶ Make sure you are learning key vocabulary for each topic area, so that whichever subject comes up you will have some impressive words to use.

Vocabulary

▶ Learn lists of words regularly and build in time to go back over words you learned a week or two ago. Reinforcement makes them stick!

▶ Choose a system of recording new words which works for you. It could be paper lists, small sections on individual cards, recording the words and their English meanings on tape, making posters to stick on your bedroom wall ... what's important is that you are noting the words and going over them regularly!

▶ You were probably encouraged to use a good range of vocabulary in the essays you wrote during the year. Go back over them, highlighting good words and phrases and writing the English in the margin, then use this to test yourself. Words are often easier to learn in context.

Grammar

▶ Keep doing practice exercises in areas where you know you are weak.

▶ Use reading texts to practise thinking grammatically. For example, highlight a selection of adjectives, then write out the English for the phrases in which they appear. Test yourself by reproducing the German phrases accurately, complete with all the correct agreements!

▶ Keep learning from your verb tables until you know all the forms of each tense of regular verbs and the most common irregular verbs. Test yourself using a die. 1 = *ich*, 2 = *du*, 3 = *er/sie/es*, 4 = *wir*, 5 = *ihr*, 6 = *Sie/sie*. Use a verb list: choose an infinitive and a tense at random, throw the die and say the correct form of the verb. Practise until you can do it without hesitation.

The Speaking Test: what you need to know

The test has two parts: a role play and a discussion of the topics you have studied.

Role Play (5–6 minutes) 30 marks

You will be given a stimulus sheet in English, with information on it which you will need to convey to a German person played by the examiner.

▶ The examiner will start by introducing the situation, then you will have to ask certain questions and also answer the examiner's questions, referring to the stimulus sheet for the information.

▶ The last questions will ask for your opinion on some aspect of the topic. Listen carefully to what is asked and answer it fully, giving reasons for your opinion.

▶ You are allowed to make notes. Don't write out exactly what you will say, but do note some useful vocabulary.

To do well on this section you need to respond to what you are asked and give all the relevant details on each point. When asked for your opinion, make sure you give reasons and examples to justify it. Your knowledge of grammar is also important – try to use some of the vocabulary and structures you have learned during the AS course, but stick to those you feel you can use fairly accurately. Think carefully about the role you are playing and the situation and decide whether you should address the examiner as "du" or "Sie".

Discussion of Topics (9–10 minutes) 30 marks

You will choose one sub-topic from the list on page 4 (for example 'Leisure activities' or 'Communication technology'). First, decide what aspect you wish to focus on and choose an appropriate title. Then, write five headings to indicate what areas you would like to discuss. The topic should be discussed in a German context, not a general one, so make sure you have facts and examples from German life. If you prefer, you can discuss a German literary text which you have read. You can use an A4 page of notes in German for reference.

This section is marked on four aspects:

▶ your ideas and opinions and their relevance to German culture.

▶ your fluency and ability to answer questions on the spot, without relying on pre-learned material.

▶ the quality of your language, in terms of good vocabulary and structures and also of accuracy.

▶ your pronunciation and intonation.

Turn to page 23 to see how the Speaking Test is marked.

The Family

Note to the candidate: You should begin by asking the two questions. The task can then be completed in the order you prefer. You should base your replies on the English text, but sometimes you will need to use your imagination and initiative to react to the examiner's comments and questions.

Die Situation

Sie wohnen in der Stadtmitte von Newcastle. Ihr deutscher Briefpartner/ Ihre deutsche Briefpartnerin besucht Sie in den Osterferien.

Die Aufgabe

Der Briefpartner/Die Briefpartnerin (der Prüfer/die Prüferin) will etwas mit der Familie unternehmen. Er/Sie bittet Sie um Vorschläge. Erklären Sie die Möglichkeiten mit Hilfe der Broschüre.

Zuerst müssen Sie folgende Informationen herausfinden:
  1 was genau er/sie machen möchte
  2 wie seine Familie normalerweise den Abend verbringt

Sie schlagen ein Spiel vor. Sie müssen erklären:
  • die Gründe, warum man ein Spiel am besten spielt
  • das ‚Mensch Ärgere Dich Nicht'-Spiel
  • das ‚Schlangen und Leiter'-Spiel
  • das ‚Backgammon'-Spiel
  • was am Abend am wichtigsten ist.

Im Laufe des Gesprächs besprechen Sie auch:
  • in welcher Reihenfolge man die Spiele spielen sollte
  • was man sonst noch am Abend machen könnte.

Ein paar Hilfsvokabeln:
  compendium – *Sammlung*   dice – *Würfel*   to throw a dice – *würfeln*
  board – *Spielbrett*   piece – *Spielmarke*   knocked out – *rausgeworfen*
  arranged – *aufgestellt*   opposite direction – *entgegengesetzte Richtung*

Prepare detailed answers to the questions. Look at these answers. They get better as they get fuller and more detailed. Remember to use the German vocabulary given on the sheet to help you:

▶ Es gibt drei Spiele, und es gibt drei Gründe, warum man ein Spiel am besten spielt.

▶ Es gibt drei Spiele in der Spielsammlung: Mensch Ärgere Dich Nicht, Schlangen und Leiter und Backgammon. Es gibt drei Gründe, warum man ein Spiel am besten spielt: man kann sprechen, lachen und zusammen sein.

▶ Es gibt drei Spiele in der Spielsammlung: Mensch Ärgere Dich Nicht, Schlangen und Leiter und Backgammon. Zwei von diesen Spielen sind für die ganze Familie. Man kann viel Spaß zusammen haben, und es ist besser als fernsehen. Es gibt drei Gründe, warum man ein Spiel am besten spielt: man kann sprechen, lachen und zusammen sein, und das ist wichtig als Familie.

Games Compendium – The Rules

There are three great games in this compendium and therefore three fantastic reasons to spend the evening playing as a family. It's a great way to enjoy the evening talking, laughing and being together.

Ludo
A dice game for four. Players move their pieces round the board and to the middle while trying to knock out other people's pieces.

Snakes and Ladders
Players throw a die and move their piece round a 100-square board, moving up ladders and down snakes. The winner is the first person to reach 100.

Backgammon
A dice game for two players. Throw the highest number to start. Players move their pieces round the board in opposite directions, each aiming to reach home first. Pieces can be knocked out by the opposing player.

And remember it's all about spending the evening together!

Read and listen to this student's answers to the five questions from the Speaking Test. CD Track 1

Wann spielt man am besten ein Spiel?

Man spielt Spiele am besten am Abend, weil man auf diese Weise Zeit mit der Familie zusammen verbringt. Man kann dabei zusammen lachen und reden, und man lernt sich besser kennen. Es ist gut, wenn man Zeit als Familie verbringt, weil es die Familie näher bringt.

Erkläre mir das Spiel ‚Mensch Ärgere Dich Nicht'.

Also, bei diesem Spiel muss man die Spielfiguren auf die vier Felder ihrer Farbe bringen. Die vier Spieler würfeln und bewegen ihre Spielfigur. Man kann andere rauswerfen und zurückschicken. Ich finde das Spiel toll, weil es echt viel Spaß macht.

Erkläre mir das Spiel ‚Schlangen und Leiter'.

Hier würfelt jeder Spieler und rückt auf dem Spielbrett vor. Man muss das 100-Feld erreichen. Bei einer Leiter muss man hinaufsteigen. Bei einer Schlange fällt man herunter. Ich finde das Spiel mit der ganzen Familie sehr lustig.

Erkläre mir das Spiel ‚Backgammon'.

Dieses Spiel können nur zwei Spieler spielen. Man muss mit den Spielsteinen die Heimfelder erreichen. Die Spielmarken werden auf die gegenüberliegenden Zacken gesetzt. Am Anfang müssen die Spieler würfeln, und wer die höchste Zahl hat, fängt an. Die Spieler spielen in entgegengesetzten Richtungen. Man kann die Spielsteine auch rauswerfen. Ich finde, dieses Spiel ist kompliziert.

Was findest du am wichtigsten am Abend?

Ich finde, das Wichtigste ist, zusammen zu sein und Zeit mit der Familie zu verbringen. Viele Familien spielen am Computer oder sehen fern und reden nicht miteinander. Sie essen auch oft vor dem Fernseher. Man hat also keine Möglichkeit, sich zu unterhalten, wenn man beim Essen nicht am Tisch sitzt. Ich meine, dass man mehr als Familie unternehmen sollte. Zusammensein ist einfach wichtig.

> Remember that the examiner will take the lead and interrupt you with unexpected questions. Make sure you listen carefully and answer whatever you are asked.

Now the examiner may ask other questions on the same general topic area. Here are some examples:

- Was sind die Vorteile einer großen Familie? Und die Nachteile?
- Welche Rolle spielen die Großeltern im Leben einer modernen Familie?
- Wie siehst du das Familienleben in der Zukunft?
- Welche Freizeitmöglichkeiten gibt es für die Familie?

The conversation on topics you have studied

Aspects of Daily Life Sub-Topics

The family
- Worüber streiten sich junge Leute und Familienmitglieder?
- Was wäre Ihnen lieber: Einzelkind zu sein oder Geschwister zu haben?
- Wie wichtig ist heutzutage die Ehe?
- Wo würden Sie am liebsten wohnen?

Food, drink, health, obsessions and addictions
- Sollte die Regierung fettes Essen und ungesunde Nahrung verbieten?
- Sollte man mit 16 Alkohol kaufen und trinken dürfen?
- Was ist die schlimmste Gefahr für junge Leute – Alkohol, Tabak, oder Drogen?
- Was heißt für Sie ‚sich gesund ernähren'?

Transport
- Sollten mehr Menschen mit öffentlichen Verkehrsmitteln fahren?
- Wie wichtig wäre es, mehr Radwege zu haben?
- Fliegen wir zu oft mit dem Flugzeug in den Urlaub?
- Wie kann man die Auswirkungen auf die Umwelt reduzieren, wenn wir mehr reisen?

Leisure and Entertainment Sub-Topics

Sport
- Warum sollte man Sport treiben?
- Macht man in Ihrer Schule genug Sport ?
- Wie kann man fit bleiben, wenn man keinen Sport mag?
- Sollte man mehr Wettbewerb in der Schule fördern?

Tourism and related themes
- Wie wichtig ist Urlaub für Sie?
- Was sind die Nachteile von Tourismus?
- Was kann man während der Ferien außer Reisen machen?
- Wie haben sich die Reiseziele in letzter Zeit verändert?

Leisure activities
- Gehen Sie lieber ins Kino oder sehen Sie sich lieber eine DVD an?
- Welche Musik hören Sie gern und warum?
- Ist Ihre Kleidung ein Teil Ihrer Persönlichkeit?
- Wie hat sich die Freizeit seit der Jugend Ihrer Eltern verändert?

The conversation on topics you have studied

Remember that the examiner will respond to what you say, so be careful to introduce ideas you are happy to talk about! Here are three possible ways to begin answering the same question: *Wie wichtig ist Urlaub für Sie?*
- Für mich ist Urlaub wichtig, um Stress zu vermeiden. Zum Beispiel …
- Was mir wichtig ist, ist Zeit mit Freunden zu verbringen. Ich mag …
- Ich mag Urlaub, wo man die Umwelt respektieren kann. Daher mag ich lieber zelten und …

Communication and Media Sub-Topics

Communication technology
- Ist es nötig, dass jeder ein Handy besitzt?
- Finden Sie, dass man genug Sicherheit im Internet hat?
- Wie hat sich die Kommunikation zwischen Menschen verändert?
- Wie benutzen Sie Ihren Computer?

Media
- Meinen Sie, dass Sie zu viel Zeit vor dem Fernseher verbringen?
- Wie finden Sie Realitätssendungen wie ‚Big Brother'?
- Sollte man Werbung für Alkohol und Tabak verbieten?
- Was wären die Nachteile, wenn es keine Werbung mehr gäbe?

If you make a general statement, back it up with examples. For example, if you are discussing reality TV shows, you might say: „Realitätssendungen wie Big Brother sollten verboten werden." This has more weight if you follow it up by saying: „Zum Beispiel gab es bei der letzten Serie viel Rassismus, und das sollte man nicht im Fernsehen zeigen."

Education and Training Sub-Topics

School and school life
- Was würden Sie an Ihrer Schule ändern?
- Wie wichtig ist es, eine gute Ausbildung zu haben?
- Meinen Sie, dass man zu viel Zeit an der Schule verbringt?
- Beschreiben Sie mir Ihre ideale Universität!

Work and training
- Welche Erfahrungen in der Arbeitswelt haben Sie schon gemacht?
- Als was würden Sie am liebsten arbeiten?
- Wie gut wird man in der Schule auf die Arbeitswelt vorbereitet?

Relate your ideas to contemporary society and the cultural background of a German speaking country and include facts as well as opinions. You could choose a literary text. Remember to choose something you can speak about confidently and that interests you. You will be assessed on your ideas, opinions and their relevance, your fluency, spontaneity and responsiveness, quality of language and pronunciation and intonation. Try to record yourself speaking.

The Listening, Reading and Writing Paper

You can plan your time as you wish, but there are suggested amounts of time to spend on each section.

Listening and Writing (55 marks)

Suggested time: 1 hour

There will be about five minutes of recording altogether and you will be able to play it and pause it yourself. There will be three recordings to listen to, with a variety of question types:

► non-verbal answers such as matching activities, multiple choice questions or a gapped text with a box of words to choose from to fill the spaces.

► comprehension questions in English.

► a writing task based on the last passage, for example writing an e-mail in response to an answerphone message. There will be English prompts giving you the information you have to convey.

Reading and Writing (85 marks)

Suggested time: 1 hour 30 minutes

There will be three passages of German to read, with a variety of question types:

► non-verbal answers such as multiple choice, matching or box-ticking.

► short answers in German.

► writing a longer piece in German in response to a text, summarising some of its content and then giving your own ideas or opinions.

The key ways to prepare are by:
► learning key vocabulary for each topic area
► revising the main grammar points
► doing plenty of listening practice to keep your ear 'tuned in' to German
► practising writing summary pieces and then giving your opinion on the topic
► working through the exam-type questions and tips on the following pages.

Family

Aufgabe 1 (Teil 1)　　　CD Track 2
Listen and answer the following questions in English.

a What is Vanessa's family situation? (4)

_____

_____

_____

_____

b What does her mother think she ought to do? (2)

_____

_____

c What problem does Lukas have? (2)

_____

_____

d How does he describe his mother? (2)

_____

_____

e Describe Donata's problem! (2)

_____

_____

f What effect has this problem on her life? (2)

_____

_____

> Read questions carefully. Pay attention to marks given for each question as this is indicative of the amount of detail required.

Drei Jugendliche sprechen über ihre Familienprobleme.

Vanessa: Meine Eltern sind seit zwölf Jahren geschieden, und ich wohne mit meiner Mutter und meinem Bruder zusammen. Mein Vater hat jahrelang keinen Kontakt mit uns gehabt, aber plötzlich will er uns wieder sehen. Ich habe keine Lust, ihn kennen zu lernen, aber mein Bruder will sich mit ihm treffen. Meine Mutter meint, ich solle ihm eine Chance geben, aber es ist meine Entscheidung. Ich weiß nicht, was ich tun soll!

Lukas: Ich bin Einzelkind und vierzehn Jahre alt. Meine Mutter und ich streiten immer. Sie ist sehr ängstlich und behandelt mich wie ein kleines Kind. Sie ist immer misstrauisch und glaubt mir nie. Ich brauche mehr Selbständigkeit, aber wie schaffe ich das mit meiner Mutter?

Donata: Ich bin die zweitälteste von vier Kindern. Meine ältere Schwester ist sehr sportlich und kriegt immer gute Noten in der Schule, ich leider nicht. Mein Vater ist von mir enttäuscht und kritisiert mich ständig vor der ganzen Familie. Er macht sich auch lustig über mich, auch vor Fremden. Ich habe nicht sehr viel Selbstvertrauen, und meine Noten in der Schule werden immer schlechter. Was soll ich machen?

Aufgabe 1 (Teil 2)

Send an email IN GERMAN to a youth magazine and give your views on teenagers and family problems. (10 marks for Quality of Language and 10 marks for Communication)

Mention the following points:

- Everyone knows that teenagers have always had difficulties with their parents and other relatives.
- But today it might be worse, because there are more one-parent families and divorced parents.
- It's best to avoid quarrels over minor things like clothes, music and whether a bedroom is tidy.
- But bigger issues such as alcohol, boy- and girlfriends and education must be discussed calmly.
- Parents and teenagers all need to be willing to see the other person's point of view.

Hallo Leute!

You should ensure you provide all the information provided in the instructions in English, though be careful not to translate word for word! You will be marked on your having included all the required information, and on your accuracy. Make sure you also include a wide variety of structures, as your quality of language is also marked.

Healthy living

Aufgabe 2   CD Track 3
Hören Sie diesen Bericht und haken (√) Sie die richtige Alternative ab. (4)

a Annike findet das Lernen

langweilig

stressig

einfach

b Für Medizin braucht man

durchschnittliche Noten

niedrige Noten

sehr gute Noten

c Annike entspannt sich

sehr oft

selten

nie

d Sie isst gern

Fastfood

frische Lebensmittel

Schokolade

> Read the question and possible answers very carefully. Listen to the item very carefully. Look out for negatives and 'false friends', which could mislead you.

Annike ist Studentin und wohnt in Freiburg. Sie macht nächstes Jahr ihr Abitur und möchte dann Medizin studieren.

Annike: Ich finde mein Leben ganz schön stressig. Ich stehe jeden Morgen sehr früh auf, um meine Hausaufgaben zu machen. Ich kann mich morgens viel besser konzentrieren. Ich stehe unter viel Stress, weil man für Medizin einen höheren Notendurchschnitt braucht als für andere Fächer. Ich glaube, dass es sehr wichtig ist, auf meine Gesundheit zu achten. Ich entspanne mich regelmäßig, um mich ausgeglichener zu fühlen und intensiver lernen zu können. Ich entspanne mich am besten mit Musik oder einem langen Bad. Ich achte darauf, dass ich genug Schlaf bekomme und dass ich gesund esse. Fastfood kann ich nicht leiden. Das ist zu fettig für mich. Ich esse lieber Salate und frisches Gemüse und trinke Fruchtsäfte.

Education and Training

Aufgabe 3   CD Track 4

Hören Sie den Bericht und setzen Sie das fehlende Wort in die Lücke ein. Wählen Sie das richtige Wort aus der Liste unten. Es gibt mehr Wörter als Lücken. Benutzen Sie jedes Wort <u>nur einmal</u>. (8)

Immer mehr Jungen wollen (**a**) _____ werden, Mädchen dagegen Polizistin. Mehr als ein Viertel möchte Tierärztin, Ärztin oder Krankenschwester (**b**) _____. Zum ersten Mal tauchten (**c**) _____ auf der Liste von Jungen (4,1%) und Mädchen (1,0%) auf. Die meisten nannten eine gute Ausbildung, Computer- und (**d**) _____ als wichtige Eigenschaften – Kompetenzen, die auch in der Wunschliste von Geschäftsführern (**e**) _____. Die Umfrage nannte auch gute Kommunikationsfähigkeiten, (**f**) _____ und Teamfähigkeiten als (**g**) _____ persönliche Eigenschaften. Die Wirtschaft sucht außerdem Mitarbeiter, die (**h**) _____ Englisch sprechen und eine gute Allgemeinbildung haben.

auftauchen	Fußballer	werden	wird	Sprachen
Computerberufe	Sprachkenntnisse	positiv	Lernen	sein
wichtige	Flexibilität	fließend	Eigenschaften	
Fußball	Polizist	fehlen	schlimme	

> Use your knowledge of grammar to work out what the missing word is and then use a process of elimination and the sense of the sentence to work out which of the possible words is correct.

Arbeitsträume

Immer mehr Jungen wollen Fußballer werden. Mädchen träumen dagegen von einer Karriere als Ärztin. In einer Umfrage des Münchner Instituts für Jugendforschung erklärten 14,5% der Jungen, Kicker sei Ihr Traumjob. Auf Platz zwei kam Polizist, gefolgt von Pilot und Kfz-Mechaniker. Bei Mädchen steht der Umfrage zufolge Helfen hoch im Kurs. Mehr als ein Viertel möchte Tierärztin, Ärztin oder Krankenschwester werden. Model oder Schauspielerin liegen bei den Berufswünschen der Mädchen erst hinter Polizistin oder Lehrerin. Zum ersten Mal tauchten Computerberufe auf der Liste von Jungen (4,1%) und Mädchen (1,0%) auf. Und welche Kompetenzen werden sie in der künftigen Arbeitswelt brauchen? Die meisten nannten eine gute Ausbildung, Computer- und Sprachkenntnisse als wichtige Eigenschaften – Kompetenzen, die auch in der Wunschliste von Geschäftsführern auftauchen. Die Umfrage nannte auch gute Kommunikationsfähigkeiten, Flexibilität und Teamfähigkeiten als wichtige persönliche Eigenschaften. Die Wirtschaft sucht außerdem Mitarbeiter, die fließend Englisch sprechen und eine gute Allgemeinbildung haben. "Bloß keine Fachidioten, die nichts anderes im Kopf haben", meinte der Direktor eines großen Kölner Medienhauses.

Aufgabe 4
Lesen Sie diesen Artikel.

Interviewer: Hallo von Jugend heute! Wir hören immer, dass es viel zu viel Werbung im Fernsehen, im Radio und auf den Straßen gibt. Die Frage: Sollte man alle Werbung verbieten? Wir haben drei Studenten aus Berlin nach ihrer Meinung gefragt.

Hallo, Marianne. Was können Sie zu diesem Thema sagen?

Marianne: Also, ich glaube, Werbung kann schon nützlich sein. Die Werbung informiert uns alle über neue Produkte und Sonderangebote. Teilweise gibt es aber zu viel Werbung, besonders die an Kinder gerichtete Werbung. Kinder sind sehr leicht zu beeinflussen, und das bereitet Probleme für die Eltern. Ich würde alle Werbung im Fernsehen verbieten, wenn Kindersendungen laufen.

Interviewer: Und Sie, Peter, was sagen Sie dazu?

Peter: Ohne Werbung gibt es Schwierigkeiten für Firmen, uns auf ihre Produkte aufmerksam zu machen. Da wir in einer Konsumgesellschaft leben, ist die Werbung unentbehrlich. Anstatt alle Werbung zu verbieten, würde ich lieber den Inhalt kontrollieren, um Stereotypen abzubauen.

Interviewer: Und zuletzt Jessica. Würden Sie Werbung verbieten?

Jessica: Ich würde sehr gern Werbung im Fernsehen verbieten. Werbung stört immer, wenn ich einen Film angucke. Ich möchte gern einmal in Ruhe fernsehen. Werbung kann auch sehr gefährlich sein, da sie ein ideales Weltbild darstellt und sehr verführerisch sein kann. Das ist nichts anderes als Gehirnwäsche, besonders für junge Leute.

Welche der drei Gefragten ist das? Marianne (M), Peter (P) oder Jessica (J)? Schreiben Sie jedes Mal einen Buchstaben ins Kästchen.

Wer sagt ...?

a Werbung ist eine Art Manipulierung.

b Werbung informiert uns über neue Produkte.

c Eine freie Marktwirtschaft braucht Werbung.

d Werbung ist unrealistisch.

e Man sollte Werbung für bestimmte Produkte verbieten.

> Look out for synonyms – different ways of describing the same thing.
> Read statements very carefully.

Aufgabe 5
Lesen Sie den folgenden Artikel und beantworten Sie die Fragen
AUF DEUTSCH (25 Punkte: 15 für Verständnis des Textes und 10 für
Qualität der Sprache)

Stress, Herzkrankheiten, Abhängigkeiten von verschiedenen Drogen
(Tabak, Alkohol usw.) Krebs – diese Krankheiten unserer Zeit kann man
vermeiden. Man muss nur bereit sein, seinen ungesunden Lebensstil zu
ändern. Eine ausgeglichene Ernährung mit vielen Vitaminen kann den
Cholesterinspiegel reduzieren und vor Herzinfarkt schützen.

Der moderne Mensch steht häufig unter Stress. Man füllt seine Tage
mit immer mehr Aktivitäten, nimmt sich aber nicht mehr Zeit dafür.
Entspannung, Yoga und Meditation können helfen, Stress abzubauen.
Eine neue Art sich zu entspannen ist ‚Stopping'. Man bekommt
praktische Ratschläge, wie man die Dinge erkennen kann, die wirklich
wichtig sind. Aber auch ‚Stopping' kann nur wirksam sein, wenn man
bereit ist, einige Sachen, die man vielleicht geniesst, aufzugeben.

a Was sind die Krankheiten unserer Zeit? (2)

_____

b Wie kann man so genannte Zeitkrankheiten vermeiden? (2)

_____

c Warum ist eine ausgeglichene Ernährung wichtig? (3)

_____

_____

d Warum gibt es so viel Stress im Leben? (2)

_____

e Wie kann man den Druck reduzieren? (3)

_____

_____

f Wie funktionert ‚Stopping'? (2)

_____

g Was muss man tun, damit ‚Stopping' wirklich helfen kann?

> Use the language of the questions and the text and reword the answers
> using your knowledge of German grammar.

Aufgabe 6
Lesen Sie den folgenden Text und beantworten Sie die Fragen AUF DEUTSCH. Schreiben Sie ungefähr 300 Wörter. Sie sollten dabei keine Wortreihen kopieren. Wenn Sie mehr als fünf Wörter kopieren, werden Sie Punkte verlieren.

Hausaufgaben online!

Vor einem Jahr ging der 19-jährige Gymnasiast Bastian Wilhelm aus Celle mit seinem Hausaufgaben-Service online. www.cheat.ne.de bietet jede Menge Referate und Stoffsammlungen zu den verschiedensten Themen.

Die Idee enstand vor etwa drei Jahren, als Bastian bei einem seiner ersten Surfs feststellen musste, dass es online kaum etwas Interessantes und Brauchbares für Schüler gab.

Die Zeit spielt eine wichtige Rolle für Bastian. Er arbeitet täglich an seiner Internetseite, aber er sieht im Computer nur ein Mittel, um Zeit zu sparen.

Die Reaktionen auf sein cheat.net waren bisher hauptsächlich positiv. Sein Vater, der selbst Rektor ist, hält den Service für eine ‚wunderbare' Möglichkeit zum Recherchieren. Wunderbar finden diese Projekte aber vor allem die Schüler.

Auf Deutsch heißt „cheat" zwar so viel wie Betrug oder Schwindel, doch das ist nicht die Grundidee der Seite. „Wer die Infos herunterlädt, ohne seinen Kopf einzusetzen und das Material nachzuprüfen, ist selbst Schuld", sagt Bastian. „Denn nicht alles, was im Internet steht, ist wahr."

(a) Ihre Antwort zu dieser Frage sollte auf dem Text basieren:

Warum hat Bastian diese Webseite gebaut und wie finden es andere Leute? **(Verständnis des Textes: 10 Punkte)**

(b) Schreiben Sie jetzt Ihre eigenen Ideen zum Internet:

Wie benutzen Sie das Internet hauptsächlich? Zum Recherchieren oder zum Zeitvertreib? Warum?
(Persönliche Ansicht: 20 Punkte/Qualität der Sprache: 20 Punkte/ Total: 50 Punkte)

Aufgabe 1 (Teil 2)

When attempting any written questions like in Aufgabe 1 (Teil 2), you are being graded on your communication and your accuracy only. It is therefore important that you read through the question carefully and write the information in German. You should not translate each word, but do make sure you fulfil each task. When writing in German, it is wise to stick to language and structures you are confident with, but ensuring a range of structures, tenses and vocabulary fit for AS.

Aufgabe 6

When attempting any of the written questions like Aufgabe 6, ensure that you read the question carefully. It is vital that you pay as much attention to the question itself as to the stimulus material.

Make a plan so that you know what you are going to write. Make sure you have a beginning, a middle and an end. Deal imaginatively with the argument, especially with question (b) and make sure that you add your own opinion and justify that opinion with examples.

With question (a), ensure you don't lift phrases from the passage, but do refer to it frequently and relevantly. With question (b), ensure you develop the points already made in the passage, but also express your own original points of view clearly.

Make sure your sentences link well, using conjunctions and relative clauses. Ensure also that you use a range of tenses. Do remember to use the first person when requested to do so by the essay question. Try to vary your language and avoid repeating phrases. Try to include idioms where possible.

Make sure that you write about 300 words, ensuring that your work is neat and legible.

Build in enough time to check your work carefully. Read through looking for specific things, i.e. read through the first time looking at just the verbs, checking tenses, agreements and positions; read through the second time looking at nouns and adjectives, looking for agreements and capital letters. Read the whole essay silently to yourself: this helps to check accuracy and flow.

Your essay will be marked for Comprehension, Response, Accuracy and Range. The grades used can be summarised as follows.

	Comprehension of texts	Response of texts	Accuracy of language	Range of language
V. good	9–10	16–20	9–10	9–10
Good	7–8	12–15	7–8	7–8
Sufficient	5–6	8–11	5–6	5–6
Limited	3–4	4–7	3–4	3–4
Poor	0–2	0–3	0–2	0–2

Examiners allocate marks to candidates' work on a best-fit basis.

The Speaking Test: Answer Marks	
Section A: Speaking – Role-play	**Answer Marks**
• Use of stimulus AO2 Grid A	**(15)**
• Response to examiner AO1 Grid B	**(10)**
• Quality of Language (Accuracy) AO3 Grid C.1	**(5)**
	Section A Total **(30)**
Section B: Speaking – Topic Discussion	**Answer Marks**
• Ideas, opinions and relevance AO1 Grid D	**(10)**
• Fluency, spontaneity, responsiveness AO1 Grid F.1	**(10)**
• Quality of Language (Accuracy) AO3 Grid C.1	**(5)**
• Pronunciation and intonation AO1 Grid G	**(5)**
	Section B Total **(30)**
	Paper Total **(60)**

Grammar Summary

1 Nouns and articles

1.1 Gender

Every German noun has a gender. There are some patterns which make learning correct genders easier:
- Nouns which refer to masculine or feminine people will have the corresponding gender e.g. *der Großvater, die Mutter*
- Nouns which end in the following are usually masculine:
  -ant -er -ich -ig -ing -ismus -ist -or
- Nouns which end as follows are usually feminine:
  -e -heit -keit -ik -in -ion -schaft -ung
- Nouns which end in the following are usually neuter:
  -chen -lein -um
- Words from other languages are also often neuter e.g. *das Hotel*
- The gender of a compound noun is always the gender of the last noun element e.g. *das Taschengeld, die Zugkarte, der Hausmann*

1.2 Definite and indefinite articles

	masc.	fem.	neut.	plural	masc.	fem.	neut.	plural
nom.	*der*	*die*	*das*	*die*	*ein*	*eine*	*ein*	*keine*
acc.	*den*	*die*	*das*	*die*	*einen*	*eine*	*ein*	*keine*
gen.	*des*	*der*	*des*	*der*	*eines*	*einer*	*eines*	*keiner*
dat.	*dem*	*der*	*dem*	*den*	*einem*	*einer*	*einem*	*keinen*

- German has a distinctive use of articles and you should be careful in instances where German uses the article and English doesn't as well as other cases where English uses the article but German doesn't.
  Die Natur ist schön.   Nature is beautiful.
  Sie ist Lehrerin.   She is a teacher.

(1) Translate into German: I live in a house. She has a brother. The book is good.

2 Prepositions and cases

2.1 Cases

The German case system helps show how a sentence fits together.
- The nominative case is used for the subject of a sentence.
  ***Der Vater** hat immer Recht!* Father is always right!
  It is always used after verbs like ***sein, werden*** and ***bleiben***.

- The accusative case is used for the object of a sentence, in certain expressions of time and after certain prepositions: ***bis, durch, entlang, für, gegen, ohne, um***

  *Kauft er **den Hund?***   Is he buying the dog?
  *Sie joggt **durch den Wald**.*   She jogs through the forest.
  ***Nächste Woche** fahre ich nach Italien.* I am going to Italy next week.

- The genitive case is used to show possession after certain prepositions: *außerhalb, innerhalb, statt, trotz, während, wegen*

  Die Filme des Jahres.   Films of the year.
  Ich wohne außerhalb der Stadt.   I live outside the town.

- The dative case is used for the indirect object of a sentence after certain prepositions: *aus, außer, bei, dank, gegenüber, mit, nach, seit, von, zu*

  Ich gebe dem Hund einen Knochen.   I give the dog a bone.
  Heute gehe ich zum Arzt.   Today I am going to the doctor.

N.B. Contractions: *bei + dem = beim, von + dem = vom, zu + der = zur, zu + dem = zum*

2.2 Dual case prepositions

Nine prepositions take either the accusative case or the dative case: *an, auf, hinter, in, neben, über, unter, vor, zwischen*

When these prepositions indicate the position of a thing or an action, they are followed by the dative case:
Er arbeitet im Supermarkt.   He works in the supermarket.

When they indicate the direction of a movement, they are followed by the accusative case:
Er geht in den Supermarkt.   He is going into the supermarket.
N.B. Contractions: *an + dem = am, an + das = ans, in + dem = im, in + das = ins*

(2) Translate into German: He is a small man. I have no idea. He has no time for his son. We're staying at home because of the bad weather. Are you writing to the sister? They are walking in the forest. They are going into the park.

3 Adjectives and adverbs

3.1 Demonstrative and interrogative adjectives

Demonstrative adjectives include: *dieser* this *jener* that *jeder* each, every
There is only one interrogative adjective, used for questions: *welcher* which
All four words follow the same declension as the definite article:

	masc.	fem.	neut.	plural
nom.	*dieser*	*diese*	*dieses*	*diese*
acc.	*diesen*	*diese*	*dieses*	*diese*
gen.	*dieses*	*dieser*	*dieses*	*dieser*
dat.	*diesem*	*dieser*	*diesem*	*diesen*

(3) Translate into German: This girl is very clever. I like that idea.

Grammar Summary

3.2 Adjective endings

Adjectives after a noun do not add any endings but when an adjective is used before a noun it has particular endings depending on the case, gender and number of the noun.

Adjective endings after the definite article, **alle, dieser** etc:

	masc.	fem.	neut.	plural
nom.	e	e	e	en
acc.	en	e	e	en
gen.	en	en	en	en
dat.	en	en	en	en

Adjective endings after the indefinite article, **kein** and the possessive adjectives:

	masc.	fem.	neut.	plural
nom.	er	e	es	en
acc.	en	e	es	en
gen.	en	en	en	en
dat.	en	en	en	en

Adjectives used without an article or other defining word, e.g after a number:

	masc.	fem.	neut.	plural
nom.	er	e	es	e
acc.	en	e	es	e
gen.	en	er	en	er
dat.	em	er	em	en

4 Translate into German: The boy is clever. I hate black coffee. I spoke to the pretty girl. He is wearing a black coat.

3.3 Adverbs

Adverbs describe **how** something is done – well, badly, efficiently. In English they usually end in '-ly' although there are exceptions such as 'well' and 'fast'.

- In German any adjective can be used as an adverb without alteration: *langsam* slowly
- There are adverbs of place describing the place where something happens: *hier* here
- Adverbs of time describe when something took place: *selten* rarely
- Adverbial phrases such as *mit Eile* quickly
- Interrogative adverbs ask where and when etc something happens: *wann* when

5 Translate into German: He drove quickly. She smiled happily.

3.4 Comparison of adjectives

Comparatives are used to compare two things using the same adjective, while superlatives compare three or more things to each other again using the same adjective.

Comparatives are formed using the adjective, adding -er and adding the appropriate adjective ending: **klein** small **kleiner** smaller
When comparing two things **als** in German translates the English 'than'.

To form the superlative **-(e)s**t is added to the adjective, followed by the appropriate adjective ending: das **billigste** Auto the cheapest car

Some adjectives add an umlaut when forming comparatives and superlatives, and some are irregular:

adjective	comparative	superlative
lang	*länger*	*(das) längste*
warm	*wärmer*	*(das) wärmste*
groß	*größer*	*(das) größte*
gesund	*gesünder*	*(das) gesündeste*
gut	*besser*	*(das) beste*
hoch	*höher*	*(das) höchste*
nah	*näher*	*(das) nächste*

6 Put a comparative adjective in each gap to complete the sentence:
Die Schule ist stressig aber die Arbeit ist noch _____.
Schokolade ist schlecht für die Gesundheit aber Fastfood ist noch_____.

3.5 Comparison of adverbs

These follow a very similar pattern to those of adjectives when forming comparatives and superlatives.

schnell	quickly	*einfach*	easily
schneller	more quickly	*einfacher*	more easily
am schnellsten	most quickly	*am einfachsten*	most easily

Irregular adverb comparisons:

adverb	comparative	superlative
gern	*lieber*	*am liebsten*
gut	*besser*	*am besten*
viel	*mehr*	*am meisten*
bald	*eher*	*am ehesten*

7 Wer ist _____, die Deutschen oder die Engländer?
(*friendlier*) Zum Frühstück essen die Engländer_____.
(*more healthily*)

Grammar Summary

4 Pronouns

4.1 Modes of address

There are three words for "you" in German:
- **du** for one person you know very well
- **ihr** for more than one person you know very well
- **Sie** for one or more people older than yourself, and people in authority

8 Translate into German "Are you coming to the cinema tonight?" using all three modes of address.

4.2 Personal pronouns

These alter according to case:

nom.	acc.	dat.	nom.	acc.	dat.
ich	mich	mir	wir	uns	uns
du	dich	dir	ihr	euch	euch
er	ihn	ihm	sie	sie	ihnen
sie	sie	ihr	Sie	Sie	Ihnen
es	es	ihm			

9 Fill the gaps with the correct pronouns: Gib _____ deine Hand. (*me*) Ich sehe _____ mindestens zweimal am Tag. (*her*) Ich kann _____ nicht finden. (*him*)

4.3 Reflexive pronouns

Reflexive pronouns are used with reflexive verbs to mean "myself" etc and are used in the accusative and dative cases as follows:

nom.	acc.	dat.	nom.	acc.	dat.
ich	mich	mir	wir	uns	uns
du	dich	dir	ihr	euch	euch
er/sie/es/man	sich	sich	sie	sich	sich
			Sie	sich	sich

10 Insert the appropriate reflexive pronoun: Wie oft duschst du _____ _____? Wo befindet _____ die nächste Post? Ich wasche _____ die Hände.

4.4 Relative pronouns

These mean 'who' or 'which/that' and they join simple sentences together. These exist for each gender and case:

	masc.	fem.	neut.	plural
nom.	der	die	das	die
acc.	den	die	das	die

gen.	*dessen*	*deren*	*dessen*	*deren*
dat.	*dem*	*der*	*dem*	*denen*

- The relative pronoun agrees in gender and number with the noun to which it refers.
- It takes its case from the role it plays within the relative clause.
- It must have a comma before it.
- It sends the verb to the end of the clause.
- It can be missed out in English but not in German.
- After **alles, viel, manches, nichts, allerlei** and the superlatives, the relative pronoun **was** is used instead.
- If the relative pronoun refers to the whole of the other clause, **was** is used again.

11 Translate into German: The teacher who teaches Latin is funny. The café that sells good coffee is expensive.

4.5 Possessive pronouns

Possessive adjectives can be used as pronouns (without a noun) and the forms are the same as for possessive adjectives, except that the masculine ends in **-er** in the nominative, and the neuter nominative and accusative end in **-es**.

Possessive pronouns take their gender from the noun to which they refer and their case from the part they play in the clause or sentence, e.g nominative:

masc.	fem.	neuter	plural
meiner	*meine*	*meines*	*meine*
ihrer	*ihre*	*ihres*	*ihre*

12 Translate into German: My house is bigger than yours. My garden is smaller than yours.

4.6 Indefinite pronouns

These stand in place of nouns, but don't refer to anything definite (someone, no-one):
jemand someone **niemand** no-one **einer** one **keiner** no-one
jeder each **man** one **etwas** something **nichts** nothing

jemand and **niemand** add **-en** in the accusative and **-em** in the dative while **einer, keiner** and **jeder** decline like **dieser** (3.2).
man is widely used in German but only in the nominative.
etwas and **nichts** do not change whatever case they are in.

13 Translate into German: nothing good, something interesting, no-one knows

Grammar Summary

4.7 Interrogative pronouns

The interrogative pronoun **wer** refers to people and declines as follows:

nom.	*wer*	**acc.**	*wen*	**gen.**	*wessen*	**dat.**	*wem*

When referring to things, German uses:

nom.	*was*		**gen.**	*wessen*
acc.	*was or wo-/wor- + preposition* *e.g. wodurch/woran*		**dat.**	*wo/wor- + preposition* *e.g. womit/worauf*

(14) Fill in the gaps: _____ ist das? _____ hast du im Kino gesehen?

5   Verbs – the basics

5.1 Reflexive verbs

Reflexive verbs are used with the reflexive pronouns (4.3). Many verbs are reflexive in German but not in English: **sich waschen**   to have a wash

Many reflexive verbs are to do with actions done to yourself, but this need not be the case: **sich etwas überlegen**   to consider something

Reflexive verbs normally take the accusative pronoun but they can use the dative pronoun if there is another direct object in the sentence. acc: *ich wasche mich*   dat: *ich bürste mir die Haare*

5.2 Impersonal verbs and verbs with a dative object

Some verbs are often used with *es* as an indefinite subject.

Gefällt es dir hier?	Do you like it here?
Es gibt ...	there is/ there are
Es kommt darauf an ...	It depends on ...
Es geht ihm gut.	He is well.
Hat es geschmeckt?	Did you enjoy it? (food)
Es tut mir leid.	I am sorry.
Es ist mir kalt.	I am cold.
Es gelingt ihm, ... zu + inf.	He succeeds in ...ing

Many idiomatic verbs take a dative object (4.2).

Es fehlt mir sehr.	I really miss it.
Das Bein tut mir weh.	My leg hurts.
Das Kleid steht Ihnen gut.	The dress suits you.
Die Hose passt ihm nicht.	The trousers don't fit him.
Das Buch gehört meiner Mutter.	The book belongs to my mother.
Das Bild gefällt ihm.	He likes the picture.

5.3 Separable and inseparable verbs

There are a few prefixes in German which are inseparable and cannot be split from the verb: **be- ent- ge- ver- emp- er- miss-   zer-** The stress in these verbs is in on the second syllable.

Most other prefixes are separable and go to the end of the clause or sentence. In the infinitive the prefix is stressed.

A few prefixes are separable in some verbs and not in others.

durch   um   unter   wider   über   wieder

5.4 Modal verbs

German has six modal verbs. They work with the infinitive of another verb which goes to the end of the sentence.

dürfen	to be allowed to	**müssen**	to have to
können	to be able to	**sollen**	to be supposed to
mögen	to like	**wollen**	to want to

6 The main tenses

6.1 The present tense

The present tense in German has three translations in English. It describes actions which are happening in the present, actions which are happening now on a regular basis as well as actions which will happen in the near future.

wissen, the auxiliary verbs and the modal verbs are very irregular and need to be learned separately:

wissen	*sein*	*haben*	*werden*
ich weiß	*ich bin*	*ich habe*	*ich werde*
du weißt	*du bist*	*du hast*	*du wirst*
er/sie weiß	*er/sie ist*	*er/sie hat*	*er/sie wird*
wir wissen	*wir sind*	*wir haben*	*wir werden*
ihr wisst	*ihr seid*	*ihr habt*	*ihr werdet*
sie/Sie wissen	*sie/Sie sind*	*sie/Sie haben*	*sie/Sie werden*

dürfen	*können*	*mögen*	*müssen*	*sollen*	*wollen*
ich darf	*ich kann*	*ich mag*	*ich muss*	*ich soll*	*ich will*
du darfst	*du kannst*	*du magst*	*du musst*	*du sollst*	*du willst*
er/sie darf	*er/sie kann*	*er/sie mag*	*er/sie musst*	*er soll*	*er/sie will*
wir dürfen	*wir können*	*wir mögen*	*wir müssen*	*wir sollen*	*wir wollen*
ihr dürft	*ihr könnt*	*ihr mögt*	*ihr müsst*	*ihr sollt*	*ihr wollt*
sie/Sie dürfen	*sie/Sie können*	*sie/Sie mögen*	*sie/Sie müssen*	*sie/Sie sollen*	*sie/Sie wollen*

6.2 The perfect tense

The perfect tense in German is used in speech to describe actions which happened in the past. It can be translated by the English simple past (I did) or by the English perfect tense (I have done).

Most verbs form their perfect tense with the present tense of the auxiliary verb ***haben*** and a past participle. ***haben*** takes the normal verb position, while the past participle goes to the end of the clause or the sentence.

Grammar Summary

- weak verbs form their past participle from the normal verb stem with the prefix **ge-** and the ending **-t** (*gemacht, gekauft)*
- mixed verbs and modal verbs change the stem but the prefix endings remain the same (***bringen – gebracht, denken – gedacht***)
- the past participle of strong verbs often have a changed stem, and take the **ge-** prefix and an **-en** ending (*gegessen, gesungen, getrunken*)
- the past participle of the auxiliaries are as follows:
  sein **gewesen** haben **gehabt** werden **geworden**
- verbs with separable prefixes insert **ge-** after the prefix (*eingekauft, aufgeschrieben, nachgedacht*) and verbs with inseparable prefixes do not use the **ge** at all (***bekommen, erreicht, missverstanden, verbracht***)

Certain verbs, which have no object, use the auxiliary verb **sein** to form the perfect tense. The majority of these verbs are strong/irregular verbs.

- Verbs of motion: *gehen   fahren   aufstehen*
- Verbs expressing a change in state or emotion:
  aufwachen   werden   wachsen   einschlafen
- Other verbs: *bleiben   sein*

The past participles of modal verbs are as follows:
dürfen **gedurft** *müssen* **gemusst** *können* **gekonnt**
sollen **gesollt** *mögen* **gemocht** *wollen* **gewollt**
But when a modal verb is used with another verb in the infinitive, the perfect tense is formed with the infinitive of the modal verb rather than the past participle. ***Sehen, hören*** and ***lassen*** behave like modal verbs and use the infinitive in the perfect tense.

6.3 The imperfect tense

German uses the imperfect tense to describe past events in writing for narrative, reports and accounts. Regular/weak verbs form the imperfect tense by adding certain endings to the stem of the verb:

*ich spiel**te**, wir spiel**ten**, du spiel**test**, ihr spiel**tet**, er/sie spiel**te**, sie/Sie spiel**ten***
If the stem of the verb ends in **-t** or several consonants an extra **e** is added: **arbeitete, trocknete.**
Strong verbs form this tense by changing the stem and these verbs need to be learned individually. They also add these endings:

ich	no ending	wir	**-en**
du	**-st**	ihr	**-t**
er/sie	no ending	sie/Sie	**-en**

e.g. gehen – ich ging, trinken – ich trank, lesen – ich las

Mixed verbs change their stem as strong verbs do but add the weak verb endings: *bringen – ich brachte, nennen – ich nannte, denken – ich dachte*

Modal verbs work like mixed verbs in that they add the same endings as weak verbs but mostly change the stem:
dürfen – ich durfte, müssen – ich musste, können – ich konnte, sollen – ich sollte, mögen – ich mochte, wollen – ich wollte

The auxiliary verbs in the imperfect tense:

sein	*haben*	*werden*
ich war	*ich hatte*	*ich wurde*
du warst	*du hattest*	*du wurdest*
er/sie war	*er/sie hatte*	*er/sie wurde*
wir waren	*wir hatten*	*wir wurden*
ihr wart	*ihr hattet*	*ihr wurdet*
sie/Sie waren	*sie/Sie hatten*	*sie/Sie wurden*

6.4 The pluperfect tense

The pluperfect tense is used to express something that had happened before something else. It is formed by combining the imperfect tense of the auxiliary verb with the past participle.
sprechen – ich hatte gesprochen
fahren – ich war gefahren

6.5 The future tense

The present tense is often used to describe an event which will happen in the near future especially if there is an expression of time indicating future meaning. *Morgen gehe ich nach Hause.* I am going home tomorrow.

The future tense is more precise and gives emphasis to the future aspect of a statement. The future tense is formed from the present tense of **werden** plus the infinitive, which goes to the end of the sentence.
Nächstes Jahr werde ich nach Indien fahren. I am going to India next year.

(15) Translate into German: I get up. *(present)* We flew to Zurich. *(perfect)* We were quite poor. *(imperfect)* I had received a book. *(pluperfect)* We will go to university. *(future)*

7 Conjunctions and word order

7.1 Word order in main clauses

The verb in German must always be the second idea in a main clause. Any phrase describing time, manner or place can begin a sentence but the verb must still remain in second place followed by the subject. Phrases have to be arranged in the order Time-Manner-Place, even if only two of the three phrases are used in a sentence.

7.2. Negative sentences

The negative adverbs **nicht** and **nie** go as close as possible to the end of the sentence but before adjectives, phrases of manner, phrases of place, infinitives, past participles and separable prefixes. **nicht** can also go before words where a special emphasis is necessary.

Grammar Summary

7.3 Questions

Questions in German are mostly expressed by inversion (swapping the subject with the verb). This inversion also happens with question words. In an **indirect question** the verb goes to the end of the clause.

7.4 Conjunctions

These co-ordinating conjunctions **do not** change the word order when connecting two clauses: *aber, denn, oder, sondern, und.*
sondern is usually used after a negative statement.
aber is used to express 'on the other hand'.

There are a large number of subordinating conjunctions which send the verb to the end of the clause: *als, als ob, (an)statt, bevor, bis, da, damit, dass, falls, nachdem, ob, obgleich, obwohl, seit(dem), sobald, sodass, solange, während, wenn, wie*

Some adverbs are used to link sentences together and the verb which follows inverts as normal. These are: *also, darum, deshalb, deswegen, folglich, und so*

7.5 Relative clauses

Relative clauses are subordinate clauses introduced by a relative pronoun. The verb in such a clause is sent to the end of the clause and the relative clause also has commas at each end to separate it from the end of the sentence.
Das Schloss, das wir gestern besuchten, war sehr schön. The castle we visited yesterday was very beautiful.

(16) Put these words into the correct order to form sentences:
mit meinem Freund-nach Italien-letzten Sommer ich bin gefahren-mit dem Zug.
entscheiden sich-Mütter-viele Frauen-für eine Teilzeitarbeit-einmal-sie-werden.

b, d und g

Vergleichen Sie:

Bild	o**b**
blei**b**en	schrei**bt**
Deutsch	gesun**d**
dürfen	bal**d**
gut	Ta**g**
ganz	Erfol**g**

Consonants **b**, **d** and **g** are pronounced like **p**, **k** and **t** respectively when they appear at the end of a word or in front of **s** or **t**.

Üben Sie jetzt diese Sätze:

Jeden Tag gesund essen – der gute Weg zum Erfolg!
Mein deutscher Freund wird bald kommen.
Ich weiß nicht, ob er lange bleibt.

-ig, -ich, -isch

Wiederholen Sie die Adjektive:

wen**ig**	mög**lich**	prak**tisch**
bill**ig**	eigent**lich**	poli**tisch**
witz**ig**	jugend**lich**	laun**isch**
güns**tig**	schrift**lich**	erfinder**isch**

Versuchen Sie jetzt diesen Zungenbrecher:

Theoretisch ist das richtig, aber eigentlich gar nicht wichtig – beschwichtigt der ewig praktische Herr Derwisch.

s, ß, st, sp

Üben Sie diese Wörter:

Sonntag	*sein*
Stein	*Straße*
Fußball	*Spaß*
Sorge	*Pass*
Staatsangehörigkeit	*Statistik*

Zungenbrecher:

Am Sonntag sitzt sein Sohn auf der Straße in der Stadt, sonst strickt er Socken, spielt Fußball und sammelt Steine.

Pronunciation

ei, ie

Wiederholen Sie:

eins, zwei, drei
Eintracht und Zwietracht
Dienstag, Mittwoch und Freitag
schwierig
der Schweiß

Die Arbeit ist nicht schwierig, aber schweißtreibend.
Ich schreibe. Ich schrieb. Ich habe geschrieben.
Er muss sich entscheiden. Er hat sich entschieden.
Liebeslieder von Liebe und Leiden

Lange und kurze Vokale

CD Track 9

Wiederholen Sie:

langer Vokal:
  mag, Rad, Spaß, Abend, sagen
  sehr, gehen, jedes, Federball, Meter
  mir, hier, Spiel, Ziel, viel
  ohne, wohnen, so, oder, Mode
  Ruhe, Schule, Fuß, zu, nun

kurzer Vokal:
  hallo, etwas, Geschmack, Stadt, satt
  Essen, Tennis, schlecht, Welt, Geld
  Gibt, sich, immer, finden, Wirkung
  kommen, besonders, Kosten, gebrochen, noch
  muss, Mutter, Eiskunstlauf, Druck, Schuss

Vokale mit Umlaut

CD Track 10

Wiederholen Sie:

schön	*erhöht*	*gewöhnlich*	*könnte*
über	*hübsch*	*Grüße*	*müsste*
Ähnlichkeit	*erwähnen*	*Fähigkeit*	*ändern*

Lesen Sie diese Wörter laut. Überprüfen Sie danach die Aussprache.

übertrieben	*Aufklärungsarbeit*	*hören*	*jeder fünfte*	*Gegensätze*
möglich	*Gefühl*	*Schönheitsideal*	*schädlich*	*fünf*
Essstörungen	*gefährlich*	*Öffentlichkeit*	*übermäßig*	*abhängig*

Zungenbrecher:

Der Mondschein schien schon schön.

-z und -zw   CD Track 11

Wiederholen Sie:

Ziel	Zug	Zaun	Zweig	Zwerg	Zweck
Einzelzimmer	jetzt	zuletzt	kurz	nützlich	
Unterstützung	Sturz	Arzt	zwanzig	gezwungen	zwölf

Hören Sie zu und wiederholen Sie:

jetzt – zuletzt
zu zweit – Zeit
kurz – Sturz
zwanzig – Zwetschgen
Zweck – Zecke

Probieren Sie diese Sätze:

Setzen Sie sich in den Zug.
Zwischen zwölf und zwei.
Zieh jetzt kurz am Seil.
Zwei Ziegen sitzen vor dem Zaun.

Zungenbrecher:

Zwischen zwei Zelten zwitschern zwölf Zaunkönige.

Compound words   CD Track 12

Wiederholen Sie:

a Gleich/geschlechtliche Partnerschaften
b Lebens/abschnitts/gefährte
a Wieder/heirat
d Geschäfts/reise
e auseinander/brechen
f Kinder/tages/stätte
g Wieder/vereinigung
h Gehirn/masse
i Wohn/gemeinschaft
j Abenteuer/lust

Vocabulary

Vocabulary learning tips

▶ Record vocabulary accurately – colour coding for genders is a very useful tool, e.g. write all masculine words in red, feminine in blue and neuter in black.

▶ Store all vocabulary in the same place. Organise a system that works for you early on. Set aside some time every week to record new vocabulary learned. Perhaps record vocabulary by topic area.

▶ Spend a few minutes every day learning vocabulary. Little and often is the key to successful vocabulary learning.

▶ Use the 'look, cover, write and check' method.

▶ Learn vocabulary from English into German as well as from German to English.

▶ Try using index cards with German on one side and English on the other and test yourself on a regular basis.

▶ Ask someone else to test you, especially out of sequence.

▶ Try to learn chunks of language in context.

▶ Group words together by writing lists of synonyms or opposites e.g. lieben/hassen, die Ehe/die Scheidung.

▶ List words in families: from the verb can you find nouns and adjectives which relate to it?

e.g	lieben	die Liebe	beliebt
	hassen	der Hass	hässlich

▶ Write out a set of words in jumbled form, then come back later and try to unjumble them. Can you sort out these eight words on the topic of smoking and drinking?

cehnaru	lakhool	ühctgis	hggiänba
maluq	boetnrev	renettgaiz	kbata

(rauchen, Alkohol, süchtig, abhängig, Qualm, verboten, Zigaretten, Tabak)

▶ Write out words with gaps for missing letters or sentences and try to complete them later. Complete these words linked to media.

Fe-nse-en   s-rfe-   -erb-ng   -edi-n   -eit-ng Z-it-chrift

(Fernsehen, surfen, Werbung, Medien, Zeitung, Zeitschrift)

General vocabulary

Time phrases

ab und zu	*now and again*
danach	*after that*
davor	*before that*
häufig	*often*
kaum	*rarely*
nach wie vor	*still*

Useful phrases

allerdings	*mind you*
alles in allem	*all in all*
als je zuvor	*than ever before*
andererseits	*on the other hand*
auf keinen Fall	*on no account*
drittens	*thirdly*
einerseits	*on the one hand*
erstens	*firstly*
hauptsächlich	*mainly*
heutzutage	*nowadays*
im Allgemeinen	*in general*
im Durchschnitt	*on average*
im Gegensatz zu	*as opposed to*
im Grunde	*basically*
im Vergleich zu	*compared with*
in der Tat	*in fact*
jedenfalls	*in any case*
keineswegs	*on no account*
möglicherweise	*possibly*
offenbar	*apparently*
ohnenhin	*anyway*
schließlich	*finally*
selbstverständlich	*obviously*
übrigens	*by the way*
umgekehrt	*vice versa*
vergeblich	*in vain*
vermutlich	*presumably*
vor allem	*above all*
wesentlich	*considerably, essentially*
zusätzlich	*additionally*
zweitens	*secondly*

Vocabulary

Presentations

Abschließend kann man sagen, dass ...	*To sum up, one can say that ...*
Einerseits ... andererseits ...	*On the one hand ... on the other ...*
Es handelt sich um ...	*It is a question of...*
Es heißt, dass ...	*It is said that ...*
Es fragt sich, ob ...	*The question is whether ...*
Im nächsten Punkt geht es um ...	*The next point deals with ...*
In diesem Kurzreferat geht es um das Thema ...	*The theme of this short speech is ...*
In diesem Kurzreferat möchte ich über ... sprechen.	*In this short speech I would like to talk about ...*
Man sieht, dass ...	*One can see that ...*
Statistiken zeigen, dass ...	*Statistics show that ...*
Zuerst spreche ich über ...	*First I will speak about ...*

Opinions

ich behaupte, dass ...	*I claim that ...*
ich bezweifle, dass...	*I doubt that ...*
ich bin der Meinung, dass ...	*I think that ...*
ich bin total dagegen	*I am completely against it*
ich bin überzeugt, dass ...	*I am convinced that ...*
ich finde, dass ...	*I find that ...*
ich gebe zu, dass ...	*I admit that ...*
ich glaube, dass ...	*I believe that ...*
ich glaube nicht unbedingt, dass ...	*I don't necessarily believe that ...*
ich habe den Eindruck, dass ...	*I have the impression that ...*
ich habe erfahren, dass ...	*I have learnt that ...*
ich hoffe, dass ...	*I hope that ...*
ich interessiere mich (nicht) für ...	*I am (not) interested in ...*
ich mache mir Sorgen um ...	*I am concerned about ...*
ich meine, dass ...	*I think that ...*
ich nehme an, dass ...	*I assume that ...*
ich schlage vor, dass ...	*I suggest that ...*
ich stimme zu, dass ...	*I agree that ...*
ich vermute, dass ...	*I suspect that ...*
die Vorteile/Nachteile sind ...	*the advantages/disadvantages are ...*
meiner Ansicht nach ...	*in my opinion ...*
meiner Meinung nach ...	*in my opinion ...*
meines Erachtens ...	*in my opinion ...*

Arguments

das beweist, dass ...	that proves that ...
das ist der Grund warum ...	that is the reason why ...
es betrifft ...	it concerns ...
es freut mich, dass ...	I am pleased that ...
es geht um ...	it's about ...
es handelt sich um ...	it's about ...
es ist fraglich, ob ...	it's questionable whether ...
es ist klar, dass ...	it's clear that ...
es ist nicht wahr, dass ...	it's not true that ...
es ist nicht zu glauben, dass ...	it's not to be believed that ...
es ist die Rede von ...	there's talk of ...
es kann sein, dass ...	it can be that ...
es kommt darauf an, was ...	it depends on what ...
es steht fest, dass ...	one thing is for sure and that is ...
es stellt sich heraus, dass ...	it turns out that ...
es stimmt nicht, dass ...	it's not true that ...
ich stimme dir (nicht) zu	I (don't) agree with you
im Gegenteil	on the contrary

Topic vocabulary

Freundschaft und Famile 1

die Ehe	marriage
die Kita (Kindertagesstätte)	nursery
auseinander brechen	to break up
erziehen (erzog, erzogen)	to raise
allein erziehende Mutter	single mother
die tödliche Krankheit	terminal illness
die Stiefgeschwister (pl.)	step-siblings
Lehrling werden	to become an apprentice
die Wiederheirat	remarriage
geschiedene Eltern	divorced parents
das Nesthäkchen	the youngest of the family
schwanger sein	to be pregnant
strahlend	sparkling
der Druck	pressure
die Zuverlässigkeit	reliability
der Sinn für Humor	sense of humour
jede Menge Zeit für andere	time for others
gegenseitige Hilfe	mutual help
der Geschmack	taste
das Vertrauen	trust
die Großzügigkeit	generosity
die Abenteuerlust	lust for adventure

Vocabulary

ähnliche Hobbys	*similar hobbies*
gemeinsamer Spaß	*fun together*
zuhören können	*to be able to listen*
die Sippe	*clan*
die Geborgenheit	*sense of belonging*
die kirchliche Trauung	*church wedding*
das Brautkleid	*wedding dress*
die Freiheit	*freedom*
gleichgeschlechtlich	*same sex*
die Scheidung	*divorce*
der Nachwuchs	*offspring*
vernachlässigen	*to neglect*
die Rente	*state pension*
die Pension	*pension from employment*

Gesundheit 2

der Qualm	*smoke*
infiziert	*infected*
beliebt	*beloved*
die Überdosis	*overdose*
erlauben	*to allow*
bewusstlos	*unconscious*
missbrauchen	*to abuse*
das Rauchen	*smoking*
schädigen	*to damage*
der Blutalkoholspiegel	*blood-alcohol level*
die Droge	*drug*
das Rauschgift	*drug*
sich spritzen	*to inject oneself*
süchtig	*addicted*
der Mut	*courage*
der Kettenraucher	*chain smoker*
das Selbstwertgefühl	*self esteem*
die Sucht	*addiction*
die Magersucht	*anorexia*
die Essstörung	*eating disorder*
der Anoretiker	*anorexic (noun)*
das Körpergewicht	*body weight*
das Abnehmen	*weight loss*
das Unterbewusstsein	*subconscious*
verstärken	*to strengthen*
verdrängen	*to repress*
die Ernährung	*nourishment, food, diet*
häufig	*common*
nachlassen	*to neglect*

versagen	*to refuse, deny*
die Ursache	*cause*
vermeiden	*to avoid*

Zu viel Information 3

die Sendung	*programme*
das Programm	*channel*
das Fernsehgerät	*television set*
sich entspannen	*to relax*
das Fernsehen	*television (concept)*
der Fernseher	*television set*
das Kabelfernsehen	*cable television*
gesättigt	*saturated*
die Gewalt	*violence*
die Kriminalität	*crime*
verherrlichen	*to glorify*
die Tatsache	*fact*
darstellen	*to portray*
verharmlosen	*to play down*
verringern	*to reduce*
die Werbung	*advertising*
beeinflussen	*to influence*
verbieten	*to forbid, to ban*
verführen	*to seduce*
der Konsumzwang	*pressure to buy*
die Gehirnwäsche	*brainwashing*
unentbehrlich	*indispensable*
verfestigen	*to reinforce*
der Werbespot	*advert*
die Boulevardzeitung	*tabloid newspaper*
objektiv	*objective*
die Sensationsmache	*sensationalism*
ausführlich	*detailed*
subjektiv	*subjective*
der Kommentar	*commentary*
der Klatsch	*gossip, scandal*
der Tratsch	*tittle-tattle*
der Zeugenbericht	*eye-witness report*
tagtäglich	*daily*
empfangen	*to receive*
die Glotze	*'the box' (slang for TV)*
rund um die Uhr	*around the clock*
der Zuschauer	*viewer*
herunterladen	*download*
gesättigt	*saturated*
die Qualität des Angebots	*the quality of what's on offer*

Vocabulary

die Staffel	*round, or series*
ausbeuten	*to exploit*
erfinderisch	*imaginative*
wahllos	*indiscriminately*
erstrebenswert	*desirable*
aufmerksam machen auf (+ Akk.)	*to make aware of*
missbrauchen	*to abuse*
berichten	*to report*
veröffentlichen	*to publish*
einschränken	*to restrict*
äußern	*to express*
ausstrahlen	*to broadcast*

Die Welt der Kommunikation 4

das Handy	*mobile phone*
die Handygebühren (pl.)	*mobile phone charges*
das Telefonat	*phone call*
SMS schicken	*to send text messages/to text*
der Internetanschluss	*internet connection*
herunterladen	*to download*
aufnehmen	*to record*
speichern	*to store*
der Bildschirm	*screen*
auftauchen	*to pop up*
der Zugang	*access*
die Recherchen (pl.)	*research*
aufladen	*to upload*
Zensur einführen	*to censor*

Freizeit 5

faulenzen	*to laze around*
Werken (pl.)	*handicrafts*
saisonbedingt	*seasonal*
die Kulturveranstaltung	*cultural event*
synchronisiert	*dubbed*
die Leinwand	*screen*
der Stummfilm	*silent film*
unterhaltend	*entertaining*
der Inhalt	*content*
der Darsteller	*performer*
der Untertitel	*subtitle*
die Vorführung	*performance*
ausländisch	*foreign*
die Kammermusik	*chamber music*
die Fotografie	*photography*

der Dichter	*poet*
der Schriftsteller	*writer*
das Gemälde	*painting*
die Skulptur	*sculpture*
das Denkmal/die Denkmäler	*monument(s)*
die Poesie	*poetry*
der Roman	*novel*
die Ausstellung	*exhibition*
der Maler	*painter*
die Oper	*opera*
das Weltkulturerbe	*world cultural inheritance*
der Dirigent	*conductor*
die Uraufführung	*premiere*

Das Alltägliche 6

ein Dach über dem Kopf	*a roof (over your head)*
das Studentenwohnheim	*student hall of residence*
die Wohngemeinschaft (WG)	*shared flat*
die Miete/mieten	*the rent/to rent*
die Obdachlosigkeit	*homelessness*
der Obdachlose/Mensch ohne Wohnsitz	*homeless person*
der Arbeitslose	*unemployed person*
die Marke	*brand*
die Werbung	*advertisement/advertising*
handeln	*to trade*
fairer) Handel	*(fair) trade*
gerecht gehandelte Produkte	*fair trade products*
der Weltladen/der Dritte-Welt-Laden	*shop selling goods from the third world*
die Entwicklungsländer	*developing countries*
(bleifreies) Benzin	*(lead-free) petrol*
der Fahrer/der Mitfahrer	*driver/passenger*
umweltfreundlich	*environmentally friendly*
umweltschädlich	*environmentally damaging*
öffentliche Verkehrsmittel	*public transport*
die Geschwindigkeit	*accident*
der (Verkehrs)unfall	*(traffic) accident*
Alkohol am Steuer	*drink-driving*
die Sicherheit	*safety*
die Welt verändern	*to change the world*
selbstständig/unabhängig	*independent*
die Wehrpflicht/die Wehrdienst	*military service*
die Zivildienst	*voluntary social service*
die Pflicht	*duty*

Vocabulary

Sport 7

die Sportart	*type of sport*
der Cholesterinwert	*cholesterol level*
das Immunsystem	*immune system*
das Herz	*heart*
die Fertiggerichte (pl.)	*ready meals*
der Schlaganfall	*stroke*
der Trendsport	*fashionable sports*
der Breitensport	*mass sport*
selbst Schuld sein	*to be one's own fault*
die Bewegung	*movement*
fördern	*to promote*
der Stoffwechsel	*metabolism*
der Kreislauf	*circulation*
der Mangel an	*lack of*
ausgewogen	*balanced*
die Empfehlung	*recommendation*
die Flüssigkeit	*fluid*
vorbeugen	*to prevent*
die Belastung	*pressure, strain*
die einzelnen Teams	*individual teams*
das Durchhaltevermögen	*perseverance*
der Teufelskreis	*vicious circle*

Tourismus 8

der Urlaub	*holiday*
die Ferien (pl.)	*holidays*
die Ruhe	*rest*
die Entspannung	*relaxation*
die Erholung	*recovery*
sich gönnen	*to allow oneself*
das Bruttoinlandsprodukt	*gross domestic product*
die Nachfrage	*demand*
die Wirtschaft	*economy*
steigen	*to rise*
zunehmen	*to increase*
die Treibhausgasemissionen (pl.)	*greenhouse gas emissions*
der Gemeinschaftssinn	*sense of community*
umweltfreundlich	*environmentally friendly*
der Arbeitsplatz	*employment*
zerstören	*to destroy*
die Reisehäufigkeit	*frequency of travel*
die Nachfrage	*demand*
sich bemühen	*to try hard*
schützen	*to protect*
erhalten	*to keep*

die Schadstoffe (pl.)	*harmful substances*
der Schwefelgehalt	*sulphur content*
belasten	*to pollute*
die Schienen (pl.)	*rail tracks*
das Verkehrsmittel	*transport*
die Besteuerung	*tax*
der Klimawandel	*climate change*

Schule und Ausbildung 9

das Abitur	*A Level (equivalent)*
sitzenbleiben	*to repeat a year*
die Grundschule	*primary school*
die Hauptschule	*secondary school (years 5–9)*
das Gymnasium	*grammar school*
die Realschule	*secondary school (years 5–10)*
die Gesamtschule	*comprehensive school*
das Internat(e)	*boarding school*
bestehen	*to pass*
durchfallen	*to fail*
die Klassenarbeit	*(written) test*
die Prüfung(en)	*exam*
das Zeugnis(se)	*report*
der Numerus clausus	*very high marks*
der Leistungskurs	*main subject*
der Kindergarten	*nursery school*
die Gleichberechtigung	*equal opportunities*
pauken	*to swot, cram*
beitragen zu	*to contribute to*
unter Druck	*under pressure*
das Selbstbewusstsein	*self confidence*
der Betrieb	*business, factory*
die Berufsausbildung	*vocational training*
das Bafög	*student grant*
(**B**undes**a**usbildungs**för**derungs**g**esetz)	
die Gebühren (pl.)	*fees*
benachteiligt	*disadvantaged*
verlangen	*to request*
klagen	*to complain*
der Durchschnitt	*average*
das Vorstellungsgespräch	*interview*
die Minderwertigkeitsgefühle (pl.)	*feelings of low self esteem*
sich bewerben	*to apply for*
unterstützen	*to support*
verzichten auf	*to do without*
der Erziehungsurlaub	*career break (to look after children)*
die Berufsaussichten(pl.)	*career prospects*

Answers

Aufgabe 1 (Teil 1)

a Vanessa's parents are divorced and she lives with her mother and brother. Her father has not been in contact for years, but suddenly wants to see them.

b Mother thinks she ought to give him a chance, but it is her decision.

c Lukas' mother treats him like a child. She does not believe him.

d Anxious/nervous and suspicious.

e Father is very critical of her and makes fun of her in front of the whole family and in front of strangers.

f She has not got much self-confidence, and her marks in school are getting worse.

Aufgabe 1 (Teil 2)

Your own answer.

Aufgabe 2

a stressing **b** sehr gute Noten **c** sehr oft **d** frische Lebensmittel

Aufgabe 3

(a) Fußballer   (b) werden   (c) Computerberufe
(d) Sprachkenntnisse   (e) auftauchen   (f) Flexibilität
(g) wichtige   (h) fließend

Aufgabe 4

a J   **b** M   **c** P   **d** J   **e** M

Aufgabe 5

a Stress, Herzkrankheiten und Drogenabhängigkeit.

b Man muss den Lebensstil ändern, damit das Leben gesünder wird.

c Wenn die Ernährung ausgeglichen ist und viele Vitamine enthält, kann sie den Cholesterinspiegel reduzieren und vor Herzinfarkt schützen.

d Man versucht, immer mehr am Tag zu schaffen, ohne sich genug Zeit dafür zu nehmen.

e Man kann sich entspannen, indem man Yoga oder Meditation treibt.

f ‚Stopping' hilft zu erkennen, was im Leben wirklich wichtig ist.

g Man muss einige Sachen aufgeben.